350+ SMART Goals and Objectives for use with Children with Autism Spectrum Disorder

2013 Edition with Integrated Helpdesk

Copyright © 2013

by Chris de Feyter M.Ed., M.Sc.

Table of Contents

To all my students:

"Thank you for teaching me
that *every* student can learn!"

Note from the Author

"Over the last 15 years, I have compiled, written, edited and authorized 1000s of SMART Goals for helping students succeed in general and special education, in Europe and North America.

What I have noticed amongst teachers is a tremendous amount of passion and willingness to help students progress through challenging times, but unfortunately many of that effort is placed in the wrong basket as no clear goal was defined.

Using SMART Goals with Objectives, or even better, with Outcomes and Indicators, educators and students have a clear go of where to work towards and what the result should look like. The SMART Goals in this book target skills that many children with an Autism Spectrum Disorder struggle with.

At the time of this writing, I am actively participating in doctoral studies, focusing on teacher retention in the special education classroom. Nevertheless, I am here to help you get your student or child to reach that goal. If you have any questions concerning a goal or if you are not sure which instructional strategy to use, use the Help Desk option in this book (see one of the last pages).

Chris de Feijter M.E.d., M.Sc.

Introduction

The work presented is a compilation of SMART Goals as created, edited, revised and gathered by the author and is subject to change and adaptation as more information is obtained.

These SMART Goals can be used as is, but better is it to revise the selected SMART Goals to accurately fit with the Current level of Performance of the student.

Most SMART Goals are written using the formula below. In some cases, a slightly different format was used.

Time – Student – Support – Skill – Accuracy and Measurement, Documentation.

(Example) By June 2015, Student X will independently be able to choose a SMART Goal from this database 100% of time, as documented in the trial logs.

This collection of SMART Goals will help educators and home schools ***jump start*** the creation of an Individual Education Plan or a Personal Program Plan. For students receiving Tier 2 interventions in a Response to Intervention Model, these goals can be used as Short-Term Objectives to guide educational programming.

Important Updates

March 2013
Now includes the highly used IEP Helpdesk feature at NO additional cost. See the last page for this great opportunity to connect to the author for feedback!

Communication

1. By June, STUDENT will demonstrate he/she is listening to classroom instruction in 4 out of 5 trials with 75% accuracy with reminders, as documented in Student's log.

2. By June, STUDENT will independently and verbally communicate her needs to the teacher, tutor, and classmates with 90% intelligibility on 4 out of 5 attempts over 5 trials, as documented in Student's log.

3. By June, STUDENT will raise his/her hand at appropriate times during instructional and non-instructional time 90% of the time on 4 out of 5 trials, as documented in Student's log.

4. By June, STUDENT will be able to independently use one complete spoken sentence to communicate with his/her teacher once daily, 90% of the time on 4 out of 5 days, as documented in Student's log.

5. By June, STUDENT will independently turn his/her head and eyes toward the speaker when directly spoken to, 80% of the time on 4/5 trials, as documented in Student's log.

6. By June, STUDENT will independently be able to communicate yes and no by nodding his/her head, 90% of the time on 4 out of 5 trials, as documented in Student's log.

7. By June, with verbal reminders from the tutor, STUDENT will demonstrate that he/she can adjust the volume of his/her voice, when inside or outside addressing Students and teachers in 7 out of 10 trials with 75% accuracy, as documented in Student's log.

8. By June, with the assistance of a tutor, STUDENT will be able to build a contact list of family members and be able to send and receive a text from a sibling, parents, and friends with 80% accuracy based on 3 out of 5 trials, as documented in Student's log.

9. By June, STUDENT will independently express his/her wants and needs inside the classroom and outside on the playground with 95% accuracy, in 4 out of 5 trials, as documented in Student's log.

10. By June, STUDENT will independently communicate with peers and teacher by carrying on a simple conversation for a minimum of 5 minutes, about a relevant topic, with 90% accuracy, in 4 out of 5 trials, as documented in Student's log.

11. By June, STUDENT will be able to independently identify and demonstrate a list of 8 different strategies one may use when they are feeling angry or upset in class, with 85% accuracy in 4 out of 5 trials, as documented in Student's log.

12. By June, STUDENT will speak in clear sentences with a minimum of 3 word phrases, without assistance, enabling peers and staff members to understand him/her with 90% accuracy on 4 out of 5 attempts, as documented in Student's log.

13. By June, STUDENT will be able to independently verbalize 20 important social sentences (from an attached list), with at least 80% accuracy on 4 out of 5 trials, as documented in Student's log.

14. By June, STUDENT will independently self-initiate a request for help from his/her teacher with minimum prompting, 4 out of 5 times over a 2 week trial, as documented in Student's log.

15. By June, STUDENT will be able to express his opinion or idea politely and independently in group discussion after listening to other classmates' ideas or opinions, at least 4 out of 5 times with 80% accuracy, as documented in Student's log.

16. By June, STUDENT will independently be able to explain the importance of taking his medications and list the possible side effect of his medication, in 4 out of 5 trials, with 90% accuracy, as documented in Student's log.

17. By June, STUDENT will be able to independently identify his own frustration level using a Likert Scale 80% of the time, in 4 out of 5 trials, as documented in Student's log.

18. By June, STUDENT will be able to express his opinion or idea politely and independently in group discussion after listening to other classmates' ideas or opinions, at least 4 out of 5 times with 80% accuracy, as documented in Student's log.

19. By June, STUDENT will independently be able to explain the importance of taking his medications and list the possible side effect of his medication, on 4 out of 5 trials, with 90% accuracy, as documented in Student's log.

20. By June, in the classroom, STUDENT will be able to, after being pre-taught a list of a minimum of 40 signed vocabulary words, use American Sign Language paired with an oral response, without tutor prompting to answer, ask a question or make a request, in 4 out of 5 trials with 80% accuracy, as documented in Student's log.

21. By June, when prompted, STUDENT will independently make a detailed comment or opinion on an issue being discussed in a small group setting, with 75% accuracy on 4 out of 5 trials, as documented in Student's log.

22. By June, with tutor support, STUDENT will demonstrate acquired English language vocabulary by speaking in simple 3 and 4 word sentences within the class setting with 80% accuracy in 8 of 10 trials, as documented in Student's log.

23. By June, STUDENT will independently be able to listen attentively to oral readings of text for enjoyment and for information, and be able to accurately answer questions involving the who, what, where, why, and how, with 80% accuracy in 4/5 trials, within a classroom or alternative setting, as documented in Student's log.

24. By June, STUDENT will independently pick out and say a single positive word from a visual chart to describe a positive experience he/she had during the day, at least 4 out of 6 times in a 6 day cycle, as documented in Student's log.

25. By June, during a 30 minute individual instructional period with a teacher or with limited tutor support, STUDENT will answer 10 simple questions on subject content using a minimum of 5 word responses in 4 of 5 trials with 80% accuracy, as documented in Student's log.

26. By June, with tutor support, STUDENT will demonstrate acquired English language vocabulary by speaking in simple 3 and 4 word sentences within the class setting with 80% accuracy in 8 of 10 trials, as documented in Student's log.

27. By June, from an adapted text, STUDENT will be able to answer independently, 4 out of 5 comprehension questions, with 60% accuracy, in 4 out of 5 trials, as documented in Student's log.

28. By June, using a subject and predicate, STUDENT will speak in sentences with a minimum of 5 words, in a classroom setting, when prompted by the teacher or tutor, with 80% accuracy in 5 out of 5 trials, as documented in Student's log.

29. By June, STUDENT will speak in simple sentences, using a minimum of 3 words to express his/her basic needs in the classroom setting with help of the teacher/tutor with 90% accuracy in 4 out of 5 trials, as documented in Student's log.

30. By June, with tutor assistance and the use of PECS cards, STUDENT will be able to use a hand signal to indicate when she wants something to eat or something to drink, 80% accuracy in 4 out of 5 trials, as documented in Student's log.

31. By June, with periodic verbal prompts, STUDENT will initiate a conversation with a peer, with 80% of the time, in 4 out of 5 trials, as documented in Student's log.

32. By June, with periodic verbal prompts, STUDENT will maintain a conversation with a peer for minimum of 1 minute, with 80% accuracy in 4 of 5 trials, as documented in Student's log.

33. By June, STUDENT will use be able to provide a matching vocalization with a series of gestures and a series of picture choices (see attached sheet), with 80% accuracy in 8 of 10 trials, as documented in Student's log.

34. By June, with occasional prompts, STUDENT will increase his/her receptive language skills by pointing accurately at a minimum of 50 individual oral words representing meaningful objects on a multiple picture worksheet, in 4 out of 5 trials with 80% accuracy, as documented in Student's log.

35. By June, with occasional prompts, STUDENT will self-correct articulation, using appropriate volume level, at least 4 out of 5 times in 4 out of 5 trials, as documented in Student's log.

36. By June, with advanced notice, STUDENT will contribute to a class discussion with a one sentence response, at least 3 out of 5 times in 4 out of 5 trials, as documented in Student's log.

37. By June, with verbal reminders from the tutor, STUDENT will perform oral motor exercises while breathing through his/her nose, with at least 60% accuracy, in 3 out of 5 trials, using a speech therapy checklist.

38. By June, with visual prompts and tutor support, STUDENT will be able to communicate his/her needs and wants when asked a question, with 80% accuracy on 4 out of 5 trials, as documented in Student's log.

39. By June, with the assistance of picture cards, STUDENT will independently be able to produce the ending sounds for b, f, l, blends, d, t, and k, in the final position, in 8 out of 10 trials with 90% accuracy, as documented in Student's log.

40. By June, STUDENT will independently use an appropriate tone of voice when talking with other peers or adults in class, 9 out of 10 times in 4 out of 5 trials, as documented in Student's log.

41. By June, STUDENT will independently wait for the teacher to call his/her name before speaking out in class 80% of the time on 4 of 5 consecutive days, as documented in Student's log.

42. By June, STUDENT will independently indicate "yes" by tapping his/her chest once, when asked a question 60% of the time in 4 out of 5 trials, as documented in Student's log.

43. By June, STUDENT will independently indicate identify correct objects by touching, when asked the name of at least 5 common objects (shirts, pants, shoes, socks, wheelchair, piano, ball, mat, orange, and banana) with 70 % accuracy on 4 out of 5 trials, as documented in Student's log.

44. By June, STUDENT will, with minimal verbal support, will increase the length of utterances to a minimum of 4 words, 80% of the time on 4 out of 5 trials, as documented in Student's log.

45. By June, with verbal prompts from the tutor, STUDENT will respond to visual presentations of a No Glamour Vocabulary Card, by answering in complete sentences, 3 of 6 questions related to qualities of objects, with at least 60% accuracy in the Vocabulary Development Checklist in 3 of 5 trials.

46. By June, STUDENT will independently answer 5 who is doing what, where type questions, asked by a tutor, with 95 % accuracy in 4 out of 5 trials, as documented in Student's log.

47. By June, with verbal correction from the resource teacher, STUDENT will orally answer at least 3 of 5 vocabulary development questions for Lingui Systems Vocabulary Cards, in complete sentences with at least 60% accuracy in the Vocabulary Development Checklist in 3 out of 5 trials.

48. By June, STUDENT will independently name and categorize 40 out of 50 objects into different categories with 95% accuracy in 4 out of 5 trials, as documented in Student's log.

49. By June, STUDENT will construct, with tutor prompts and using picture cues, 3 sentences of the pattern of Adjectives - who did what , how, and where with 80% accuracy in 4 out of 5 trials, as documented in Student's log.

50.   By June, STUDENT will independently and clearly state the names of a minimum of 30 of 40 pictures of objects on page 89 of HELP, with 100% accuracy on 3 out of 5 trials, as documented in Student's log.

51.   By June, STUDENT will independently formulate 5 sentences with picture cues, using the following sentence pattern of adjective who did what, and adverb when, where, and why with 80% accuracy in 4 out of 5 trials, as documented in Student's log.

52.   By June, STUDENT will independently tell the resource teacher how 7 of 10 people are feeling from a series of portrait pictures, with 80% accuracy in 4 out of 5 trials, as documented in Student's log.

53.   By June, STUDENT will be able to, when given 5 vocabulary works to use, independently talk about the picture presented to her, using at least 3 of the vocabulary words in at least 3 sentences, with 80% accuracy in 4 out of 5 trials, as documented in Student's log.

54.   By June, STUDENT will, in the classroom, verbally give a response of at least 1 sentence in length, at least 70% of the time with self-correct, without any prompting in 4 out of 5 trials, as documented in Student's log.

55.   By June, using 10 facial expression pictures, STUDENT will indicate to the teacher which feelings are indicated in each of the pictures, with 70% accuracy in 4 out of 5 trials, as documented in Student's log.

56.   By June, STUDENT will, when in the classroom, make requests for highly preferred items using the utterances of : I want - water - snack - book - car - paint with at least 75% accuracy in 4 out of 5 trials, as documented in Student's log.

57.   By June, STUDENT will, with tutor support, retell 6 events (telling who did what, where, and why) from a story suitable for his/her grade level, that has been read to him/her and using picture cues, 4 out of 5 days with 95% accuracy, as documented in Student's log.

58.   By June, STUDENT will voluntarily and independently tell 2 things done in school yesterday to a teacher or tutor on a daily basis, with 90% accuracy, 3 out of 4 days, as documented in Student's log.

59.   By June, using body language pictures, STUDENT will indicate to the teacher which feeling he/she identifies in pictures expressing emotion, and correctly identify emotion with an accuracy of 70 % in 7 out of 10 trials, as documented in Student's log.

60. By June, STUDENT will independently and accurately enunciate word on an articulation test (see attached test) administered by a resource teacher with 95% accuracy on 4 out of 5 trials, as documented in Student's log.

61. By June, with verbal reminders from the tutor, STUDENT will complete oral-motor exercises to decrease mouth breathing and decrease hyper nasal voice quality with at least 60% accuracy in the Speech Therapy Checklist in 3 out of 5 trials.

62. By June, STUDENT will construct 5 sentences, using the pictures and format of the Folkes Sentence Builder Kit , and with verbal prompts from a tutor, use the pattern who, did what, when, where, why and how, with 95% accuracy in 4 out of 5 trials, as documented in Student's log.

63. By June, STUDENT will be able to independently slow down rate of speech in order to produce speech sounds /s/, /sh/,/z/ and /zh/ with 85% clarity in 4 out of 5 trials, as documented in Student's log.

64. By June, when upset, with tutor prompting when needed, STUDENT will be able to express in words clearly what the Student needs or wants 100% of the time in 5 out of 5 situations, as documented in Student's log.

65. By June, STUDENT will say a minimum of 3 sentences to peers without a break in fluency, when attempting to communicate at least 60% of the time in 4 out of 5 trials, in the classroom, as documented in Student's log

66. By June, STUDENT will, when not able to convey a message orally, independently take a self-time out so that he/she can write on a piece of paper a word or phrase describing what message he/she wishes to convey and present it to the interested party, at least 70% of the time, in 4 of 5 situations, as documented in Student's log.

67. By June, when given a targeted word of the day, and when said at least 5 times during the day, STUDENT will be able to, with minimum prompting, use the word of the day to produce a short phrase or sentence in 4 out of 5 trials, as documented in Student's log.

68. By June, after hearing a tutor/teacher give a verbal cue to "stop" "use words slow", STUDENT will independently stop chattering and use a minimum of 1 real word with 90% accuracy in 4 out of 5 days, as documented in Student's log.

69. By June, when given a list of 10 pictures of words with consonant endings, STUDENT will be able to produce the final consonant sounds accurate and independently 80% of the time in 4 out of 5 trials, as documented in Student's log.

70. By June, when given 5 alliterations and 5 blending activities (from a phonemic awareness test), STUDENT will be able to answer independently and correctly 100% of the time in 4 out of 5 trials, as documented in Student's log.

71. By June, STUDENT will be able to express a demand for an object needed or wanted, by him/her using a sentence of at least 6 words, clearly with minimal prompting, 80% of the time in 4 out of 5 trials, as documented in Student's log.

72. By June, when approached by a familiar person, STUDENT will independently express in words a greeting (hello, hi, how are you), without touching the other person, 90% of the time in 4 out of 5 trials, as documented in Student's log.

73. By June, in the classroom, and at recess, STUDENT will be able to go up to a peer and request to play or partner in a set activity, without tutor or teacher prompting, 80% of the time in 4 out of 5 situations, as documented in Student's log.

74. By June, when STUDENT has spoken a sentence in a mixed up order, with the assistance of a tutor or teacher in repeating the mixed up order sentence, STUDENT will be able to restate the sentence back correctly, at least 60% of the time in 4 out of 5 situations, as documented in Student's log.

75. By June, with limited support, STUDENT will be able to express basic needs and wants using a Picture Exchange Communication System (PECS), by pointing to the appropriate pictures while verbalizing a 3 - 5 word request/response, with 90% accuracy in 4 out of 5 trials, as documented in Student's log.

76. By June, STUDENT will demonstrate understanding of prepositions, by correctly responding to oral directions to place objects (in, out, up, down, under, above, below, to) with minimal prompting, 90% of the time, in 5 out of 5 trials, as documented in Student's log.

77. By June, STUDENT will be able to and effectively communicate basic needs and wants (see attached sheet) at school, using hand signs, gestures, or PECS cards, with tutor prompting, at least 90% of the time, in 4 out of 5 trials, as documented in Student's log.

78. By June, using an assist of a green circle for "yes" and a red triangle for "no" taped on the Student's desk, STUDENT will independently and correctly respond to yes/no type questions 80% of the time in 4 out of 5 trials, as documented in Student's log.

79. By June, using visual/verbal cues and working 1:1 with the school resource teacher, STUDENT will verbally express 20 age appropriate concepts (recommended by the SLP), with 90% accuracy in 4 out of 5 trials, as documented in Student's log.

80. By June, with occasional prompts, STUDENT will demonstrate increased articulation skills in a variety of settings (classroom, lunchroom, hallways, work placement), with peers, teachers, and other adults, and be understood 60% of the time, in 4 out of 5 situations, as documented in Student's log.

81. By June, with verbal reminders from a tutor, in the classroom, STUDENT will perform oral motor exercises, while breathing through his/her nose with at least 50 % accuracy, in the Speech Therapy checklist.

82. By June, STUDENT will use a pictogram (see attached) to indicate a diaper change by pointing to the correct image, 80% of the time 4 out of 5 days, as documented in a Picture Board Tracking sheet.

83. By June, using body language pictures, STUDENT will indicate to the teacher which feelings are represented in 10 pictures, with a minimum accuracy rate of 7 out of 10, in 4 out of 5 trials, as documented in Student's log.

84. By June, STUDENT will independently pronounce a list of articulation words included on an articulation test (see attached), administered by a resource teacher with 95% accuracy in 4 out of 5 trials, as documented in Student's log.

85. By June, STUDENT will be able to independently communicate with oral English the names associated with 75 vocabulary pictures (see attached list) with 80% accuracy in 4 out of 5 trials, as documented in Student's log

86. By June, when given a conflict scenario (see attached listing of conflict scenarios), STUDENT will present effective steps toward a peaceful resolution process, as outlined on a conflict resolution checklist, 60 % of the time in 4 out of 5 trials, as documented in Student's log.

87. By June, with verbal repeats of directions from a resource teacher during on line speech therapy with a speech therapist, STUDENT will complete oral-motor exercises to decrease mouth breathing and decrease hyper nasal voice quality, with at least 60% accuracy in 3 out of 5 trials, as documented in Student's log.

88. By June, with verbal correction from the resource teacher, STUDENT will orally answer at least 3 of 7 vocabulary development questions from No Glamour

Vocabulary Cards, in complete sentences, with at least 60% accuracy in the Vocabulary Development Checklist in 3 of 5 trials.

89.   By June, STUDENT will be able to do the follow conversational conventions of: maintaining eye contact, staying on topic, asking relevant questions, answering questions accurately, and ending a conversation appropriately, with prompting only if needed, at least 70% of the time in 4 out of 5 trials, as documented in the Student's data log.

90.   By June, STUDENT will, when upset, use words to tell the teacher or tutor what is wrong, after being prompted, at least 80% of the time, as documented by the Student's data log.

91.   By June, when given a list of 20 words in the HELP program, STUDENT will be able to demonstrate an understanding of these words by using them to describe, categorize, classify, and compare, with at least 80% accuracy in 4 out of 5 trials, as documented in the Student's data log.

92.   By June, using words, gestures, and pointing at PECS cards, STUDENT will be able to express a want or need to the tutor, teacher, or peer without getting frustrated at least 70% of the time , in 4 out of 5 situations, as documented in the Student's data log.

93.   By June, STUDENT will have learned to slow down his/her rate of speech sounds /s/, /sh/, /z/, and /zh/ and achieve 75% intelligibility in spontaneous sentences containing these sounds, 80% of the time, in 4 out of 5 trials, as documented in Student's log.

94.   By June, STUDENT will accurately produce the sounds /ch/, /sh/, /s/ in the final, middle, and initial position of words, at a conversational level, 90% of the time in 4 out of 5 conversational sessions, as documented in Student's log.

95.   By June, STUDENT will be able to increase semantic word skills by demonstrating understanding of non-literal expressions (such as idioms and sarcasm) by using the expressions after being given an explanation of meaning, correctly 90% of the time in 4 out of 5 trials, as documented in the Student's log book.

96.   By June, in the classroom, STUDENT will use PECS cards to request an item or communicate a want, when given a choice of 3 cards with tutor prompting, at least 2 times per day 4 out of 5 days, as documented in Student's log.

97. By June, when STUDENT is responding in non-words, a teacher or tutor will intervene by modeling orally the appropriate word phrase, and the Student will repeat the real word phrase accurately and independently, 80% of the time in 4 out of 5 trials, as documented in Student's log.

98. By June, when given a picture to describe, and after modeling and prompting by a teacher/tutor, STUDENT will be able to expand a spoken sentence to describe the picture, by a minimum of 3 words, 90% of the time in 4 out of 5 trials, as documented in Student's log

99. By June, STUDENT will be able to produce the following sounds: 1) final p, b, m, t, d sounds in a word 2) velar sounds k, g in the final position of words 3) produce the sound j as in badger in the al position of words 4) produce the sound I in all word positions 5) produce the sound y in all word positions, at the conversational level with 90% accuracy in 4 out of 5 trials, as documented in the SLP progress reports.

100. By June, when other Students attempt to communicate 1 on 1, STUDENT will ask Students to speak into a microphone or ask for the FM sound system to be turned on to better hear the Student, 90% of the time in 4 of 5 situations, as documented in a Student's data log.

101. By June, when presented with 10 sentences read aloud, STUDENT will be able to choose the correct pronoun from a given choice of 2 pronouns, with 80% accuracy in 2 out of 3 trials, as documented in Student's log.

102. By June, after STUDENT has spoken the sentence in a mixed up order and when the sentence is repeated back, he/she will be able to independently restate the sentence back orally 80% of the time independently, as recorded in a Student's data log.

103. By June, with limited hand-over-hand guidance, and with verbal directions and visual cues (using Picture Exchange Communication pictures and/or photographs), when STUDENT is asked a question and shown and told two options, he/she will point to one of two pictures and accurately indicate his/her choice for: yes-no, eat-drink, hot-cold, walk-sit, sleep-play, with 75% accuracy in 3 out of 4 trials.

104. By June, with tutor support, a visual display of PECS pictures to be shown or pointed to, and with limited oral prompting, STUDENT will learn to communicate in 3 to 5 word sentences to play with blocks by saying "I want blocks please", to play with dough by saying " I want play dough please", to play with Lego saying " I want Lego

please", 75% of the time in 3 out of 4 trials, as documented in progress assessment results.

105.   By June, upon request from the Speech and Language Pathologist, STUDENT will have better control of oral motor muscles, by demonstrating less open mouth posture (as described in a Speech checklist) with 80% accuracy in 4 out of 5 trials, as documented in Student's log.

106.   By June, STUDENT will independently, coherently, and intelligibly express his/her opinion in a written paragraph of at least 3 sentences, with 80% accuracy in 4 out of 5 trials, as indicated in the Student's tracking log.

107.   By June, STUDENT will independently work on math related word problems for a minimum of 5 minutes in class, before asking for help from a teacher or tutor, at least 80% of the time in 4 out of 5 situations, as indicated in Student's tracking log.

108.   By June, with tutor and teacher support, STUDENT will be able to verbally produce 100 words accurately and correctly at least 90% of the time in 4 out of 5 trials, as documented in Student's log.

109.   By June, with support from a tutor or teacher, STUDENT will verbally express complete three word sentences to express basic needs and wants by saying "I want a snack, drink, bathroom, play, etc., with 90% accuracy in 4 out of 5 trials, as recording in the Student's tracking book.

110.   By June, in the classroom, the Life Skills room, and throughout the school environment, STUDENT will be able to, with tutor/teacher setting up the cards or Aug. Comm. Device, (with tutor observing with minimal verbal prompting) initiate communication through pictures and vocalizations at least 10 times per day 4 out of 5 days as documented in the Student's data log.

111.   By June, STUDENT will communicate with a peer partner by means of: 1) vocalizing and matching gestures, 2) vocalizations matched with a picture choice and 3) using an Aug. Comm. Device by pressing a switch and touching a screen, at least 80% of the time in 4 out of 5 situations, as documented in the Student's data log.

112.   By June, with occasional prompts, STUDENT will self-correct articulation errors automatically while in a conversation, in the classroom at least 60% of the time, as documented in progress assessment results.

113. By June, when given 3 items from a specific category, STUDENT will be able to add at least 3 more items that fit that category, with 90% accuracy in 4 out of 5 trials, as documented in the Student's data log.

114. By June, in the classroom, STUDENT will be able to sound out and independently organize and write a 3 sentence paragraph story, using invented spelling, if needed, and be able to read back the story, with 80% accuracy in 4 out of 5 trials, as documented in Student's log.

115. By June, STUDENT will independently compose a paragraph of 4 sentences (a topic sentence and 3 supporting detail sentences) on a topic of choice, achieving a grade of 75% or more, in 4 out of 5 trials, as documented in Student's log.

116. By June, STUDENT will independently turn his/her head and eyes toward the speaker when directly spoken to, 80% of the time on 4/5 trials, as documented in Student's log.

117. By June, STUDENT will be able to independently vocalize yes and no accurately in response to his/ her needs and wants, 90% of the time in 4 out of 5 trials, as documented in Student's log.

118. By June, with the assistance of a tutor and SLP, STUDENT will correctly pronounce k, f, g, l blends and s blends with 90% accuracy, in 4 out of 5 trials, as documented in Student's log.

119. By June, STUDENT will be able to independently hold a specific conversation discussing an outcome of a book, using complete descriptive sentences, with 90% accuracy, as documented in progress assessment results.

120. By June, STUDENT will be able to independently produce 20 important social sentences from a predetermined list, with at least 80% accuracy in 4 out of 5 trials, as documented in the Student's progress assessment.

121. By June, STUDENT will speak to express information, thoughts, and feelings in a whole or small group situation at least 80% of the time, in 4 out of 5 trials, in the context of Language Arts, or content subject areas as documented in progress assessment.

122. By June, STUDENT will independently "talk with a loud voice" when interacting with other staff or Students during the school day, 70% of the time in 4 out of 5 situations, as documented in Student's log.

123. By June, STUDENT will be able to independently speak in sentences with a minimum of 5 words in a classroom setting with peers, teachers, and tutors, 80% of the time, 5/5 days per week, as documented in progress assessments.

124. By June, when wanting a drink, STUDENT will, with tutor prompting, select the picture that represents the requested activity, 90% of the time in 5 out of 5 trials, as documented in Student's log.

125. By June, with tutor assistance and through the use of visual prompting, STUDENT will be able to indicate their need for food or drink, using a hand signal in the classroom, 60% of the time in 4/5 situations, as documented in progress assessment results.

126. By June, when given 15 basic commands using prepositions, STUDENT will be able to correctly follow these commands with no visual cues or help from his teacher with 90% accuracy in 4 out of 5 trials, as documented in Student's progress assessment.

Motor Skills / Sensory

127. By June, STUDENT will independently and legibly print in manuscript using a smooth motion 90% of the time in 4 out of 5 classes, as documented in Student's log.

128. By June, STUDENT will have experimented with 8 strategies, and will choose an effective strategy to assist him/her block out extraneous stimuli 85% of the time in 4 out of 5 trials, as documented in Student's log.

129. By June, STUDENT will independently print his name legibly using lined paper 95% of the time in 4/5 trials as documented in Student's log.

130. By June, STUDENT will independently print written journal entries legibly and neatly using lined paper 90% of the time on 4 out of 5 trials, as documented in Student's log.

131. By June, STUDENT will be able to independently hold and use a crayon to color and color for 5 minutes, 90% of the time on 4 out of 5 trials, as documented in Student's log.

132. By June, STUDENT will independently flip 20 consecutive pages in a magazine with 90% accuracy in 4 out of 5 trials, as documented in Student's log.

133. By June, with the assistance of a tutor, STUDENT will use a pair of scissors to cut and paste 3 of his/her assignments in an assignment book with an accuracy of 75% for three consecutive days over a 2 week period, as documented in Student's log.

134. By June, STUDENT will independently print on a straight line with 95% accuracy on 4 out of 5 trials, as documented in Student's log.

135. By June, STUDENT will be able to legibly write the words from his/her pre-primer Dolch sight words with the assistance of general signed exact pictures, with 90% accuracy in 4 out of 5 trials, as documented in Student's log.

136. By June, STUDENT will be able to hold a pencil independently, using a tripod grip to draw simple shapes (eg. line, X, and square) 3 out of 5 times in a two week trial as documented in Student's log.

137. By June, STUDENT with hand over hand tutor assistance, will print 10 letters (i.e. A,B,C,D,F,G,H,L,M,P)of the alphabet with 70% accuracy in 4/5 trials, as documented in Student's log.

138. By June, STUDENT will develop the ability to print all 26 letter of the alphabet on a page, 90% of the time in 5 out of 5 trials, as documented in Student's log.

139. By June, STUDENT will complete all academic activities using the necessary tech aids, when prompted by a tutor 5/5 times in 5/5 days, as documented in Student's log.

140. By June, STUDENT, with the assistance of a trained tutor, and for at least 10 minutes a day, will perform stretches, some of which involve using a Lecky Prone stander, 80% of the time in 8 of 10 trials, as documented in Student's log.

141. By June, with tutor prompting, STUDENT will successfully turn on and off the adaptive switches, with no longer than a 2 second hold down, on various personal devices, 90% of the time in 8 out of 10 trials, as documented in Student's log.

142. By June, in the classroom, STUDENT will independently wheel his/her wheelchair for a minimum of 3 feet, with teacher or tutor prompting, in 8 out of 10 trials with 90% accuracy, as documented in Student's log.

143. By June, STUDENT will independently demonstrate the use of pincer grasp, with 80% accuracy in at least 4 out of 5 trials, as documented in Student's log.

144. By the end of June, STUDENT will independently write cursive lower case letters the proper size, with no more than 1 error in every 5 lines in his written work, in 4 out of 5 writing assignments, as documented in Student's log.

145. By June, with support and supervision from the tutor, STUDENT will perform occupational therapy and physiotherapy exercises with at least 70% accuracy in 3 out of 5 trials, using an OT/PT checklist.

146. By June, STUDENT will independently turn his/her head to visually locate a "light box" 3 times out of 4 on 4 out of 5 days, as documented in Student's log.

147. By June, STUDENT will, with verbal prompts and physical support, tolerate exploring a variety of textures by touching them for at least 5 seconds on 4 out of 5 trials, before indicating he/she has had enough, at least 90% of the time in 4 out of 5 trials, as documented in Student's log.

148. By June, with intermittent support, STUDENT will maintain an upright sitting posture (head, shoulders, and hips aligned), in various sitting positions daily, for a minimum of 10 minutes per day, as documented in Student's log.

149. By June, with a stool and minimal adult support, STUDENT will climb up and down the steps on the school bus, 100% of the time on 5 out of 5 consecutive days, as documented in Student's log.

150. By June, with visual supervision from the tutor, the frequency of STUDENT's hand fidgeting behaviour will decrease as he participates in occupational therapy, with at least 60% accuracy in the Occupational Therapy Checklist in 3 out of 5 trials.

151. By June, with verbal directions from the tutor, STUDENT will complete templates for 13 of 26 upper case letters of the cursive alphabet in the Kinesthetic Handwriting Kit, with at least 60% accuracy, in the Handwriting Evaluation Checklist, in 3 out of 5 trials.

152. By June, following direct instruction from the resource teacher, STUDENT will complete pages in the Tactile Kinesthetic Handwriting Kit, which includes templates for lower case letters n-z of the cursive alphabet, with at least 60% accuracy, in the Handwriting Evaluation Checklist in 3 out of 5 trials.

153. By June, with verbal corrections from the tutor, STUDENT will complete occupational therapy exercises with at least 60% accuracy, as indicated in the Occupational Therapy Checklist in 3 out of 5 trials.

154. By June, with tutor guiding his/her hand, STUDENT will trace his/her name using lower case letters, 2 X's a day with 95% legibility in 4 out of 5 days, as documented in Student's log

155. By June, STUDENT will use a computer with adapted keyboard and tutor support, and copy 15 words from the Preprimer Dolch list with 80% accuracy 4 out of 5 days, as documented in Student's log.

156. By June, STUDENT will independently write his/her first name 4 times a day, with 100% legibility 4 out of 5 days, as documented in Student's log.

157. By June, with resource teacher supervision, STUDENT will complete at least 3 of 5 uppercase cursive handwriting practice assignments in the Tactile Kinesthetic Handwriting program with at least 60% accuracy in a handwriting evaluation checklist in 3 out of 5 trials.

158. By June, with a tutor walking beside him/her, STUDENT will walk a balance beam twice (44 ft.) each day to improve his/her balance 4 out of 5 days, as documented in Student's log.

159. By June, STUDENT will be able to independently copy 5 cursive sentences from the board in the classroom or alternative setting, making 5 errors or less, in a maximum of 20 minutes, in 4 out 5 trials, as documented in Student's log.

160. By June, STUDENT will be able to, using a keyboard, copy a note off the board which contains a minimum of 6 sentences of 8 words or less, within a maximum 10 minute time frame, with fewer than 5 mistakes, in 4 out of 5 trials, as documented in Student's log.

161. By June, using a variety of mediums (large crayon, chalk, marker), STUDENT will independently draw a variety of large shapes at least 90% of the time in 3 out of 5 trials, as documented in Student's log.

162. By June, with a tutor modeling, STUDENT will be able to blow a cotton ball with a straw the length of a table, for a minimum 5 minutes session, in 4 out of 5 trials, as documented in Student's log.

163. By June, STUDENT will be able to, using a light box, independently sort 10 items according to color, shape, sequence, and category with 80 % accuracy in 4 out of 5 trials, as documented in Student's log.

164. By June, in the classroom, STUDENT will be able to independently complete at least one strength building activity per day, for a minimum of 10 minutes, without complaint, on 4 out of 5 consecutive days, as documented in Student's log.

165. By June, when attempting to go outside and when requiring a jacket, STUDENT will be able to zip his/her own jacket up to the neck collar level, without assistance or complaints, at least 80% of the time in 4 out of 5 trials, as documented in Student's log.

166. By June, STUDENT will be able to demonstrate the following brailler skills with 70% independence in 4 out of 5 trials: a) load paper in the perkins brailler b) locate the space bar, paper grip lever, volume control, new line, enter, command, and backspace (Mountbatten) and c) locate line advance, backspace, space and return (Perkins), 80% of the time in 4 out of 5 trials, as documented in Student's log.

167. By June, STUDENT will be able to demonstrate the following Braille skills correctly and independently 80% of the time in 4 out of 5 trials a) using correct hand position

(tips of fingers), b) use 2 hands to middle of braille and then left hand to locate the beginning of the next line c) locate the shortest line and d) locate the longest line, 80% of the time on 4 out of 5 trials, as documented in Student's log.

168. By June, STUDENT will be able to independently print his/her name legibly, within the lines 90% of the time on 4 out of 5 trials, as documented in Student's log.

169. By June, STUDENT will independently be able to pick up small objects using a pincer grip, with 80% accuracy in 4 out of 5 trials, as documented in Student's log.

170. By June, STUDENT will independently print 10 words (see attached list), within the lines of loose-leaf/exercise book with a maximum of 5 letters crossing over the line, at least 80% of the time in 4 out of 5 trials, as documented in Student's log.

171. By June, STUDENT will be able to print words within the lines of an exercise scribbler a minimum of 2 sentences, and have less than 10 letters crossing over the proper lines, while using a pencil gripper, and having 3 or fewer reminders from a teacher or tutor, with 80% accuracy in 4 out of 5 trials, as documented in Student's log.

172. By June, with verbal corrections from the tutor, STUDENT will complete occupational therapy and physiotherapy exercises with at least 60% accuracy as indicated in an OT/PT Checklist in 3 out of 5 trials, as documented in Student's log.

173. By June, with peer support, STUDENT will participate in 2 - 15 minute body breaks (may include: wiggle game, ball work, muscle work, sandwich/steamroller, and scooter activities)90% of the time, in 8 out of 10 trials, as documented in progress report results.

174. By June, with verbal corrections from the tutor, STUDENT will perform physiotherapy exercises with at least 90% accuracy, as outlined in the PT Checklist, in 3 out of 5 trials.

175. By June, with verbal corrections from a tutor, STUDENT will participate in daily school activities in the senior life skills program, completing assigned occupational therapy tasks, with at least 65% accuracy, as outlined in the Energy Conservation OT Activities Checklist in 3 out of 5 trials.

176. By June, STUDENT will independently stand by his/her stander for a minimum of 5 minutes 80% of the time, 4 out of 5 days, as documented in a Log for Intensive Support.

177. By June, STUDENT will, with hand over hand support from a tutor, pick up different textured objects (Koosh balls, stress balls, and vibrating toys) with his/her hand, without placing objects in his/her mouth, 80% of the time 4 out of 5 days, as documented in a Log for Intensive Support.

178. By June, with verbal corrections from the resource teacher, STUDENT will write his/her signature in cursive handwriting from memory, with at least 50% of the Functional Cursive Handwriting Checklist achieved, in 3 out of 5 trials.

179. By June, with tutor assistance, STUDENT will complete daily deep pressure exercises and sensory exercises (see sensory material outline) recommended by an occupational therapist, 5 out of 5 days, as documented in the Student's Log for Intensive Needs.

180. By June, with verbal reminders from a teacher or tutor not to chew fingernails, STUDENT will chew on a safety straw or cap, 90% of the time in class , 4 out of 5 days, as documented in Student's log.

181. By June, STUDENT will, with prompting, be able to change a phrase into a sentence using Dolch Preprimer Phrases, with 60% accuracy in 8 out of 10 trials as documented using a Dolch Primer Tracking sheet.

182. By June, in the classroom, STUDENT will be able to complete the following recommended activities for at least 10 minutes per day: 1) stand on one leg while other foot is on a small object 2) kick a ball to tutor or peer 3) walk up and down on an uneven surface (e.g. hill, or ramp), and 4) stand on toes to reach an object 2 out of 4 days, as documented in the Student's data log.

183. By June, with tutor prompting, STUDENT will be able to independently feed him/herself using a spoon at least 60% of the time in 4 out of 5 trials as documented in the Student's data log.

184. By June, STUDENT will be able to independently, in the classroom, copy 5 cursive sentences from the board, making 5 errors or less, within a 20 minute period in 4 out of 5 trials, as documented in the Student's data log.

185. By June, STUDENT will be able to complete 10 minutes of fine motor strength building activities (as recommended by the OT) with support from a tutor, at least 3 times per week as documented in the Student's data log.

186.	By June, STUDENT will be able to independently demonstrate correct keyboarding skills by using proper hand position, 90% of the time, in 4 out of 5 trials, as documented in Student's log.

187.	By June, STUDENT will be able to demonstrate the following functions of a Mountbatton brailler: 1) locate and use the correction key 2) use the command key and at least 2 commands 3) command chord the time, with 90% independence in 4 out of 5 trials, as documented in the Student's log.

188.	By June, during Technology classes, STUDENT will independently place his/her fingers on keyboard, and type an exercise with a minimum 25 words per minute with no errors, at least 90% of the time, in 4 out of 5 typing skills trials, as documented in Student's log.

189.	By June, with tutor support, guidance, and modeling as needed, and with visual and auditory cues, STUDENT will walk to the coat rack, take his/her vest down , and with the tutor holding the vest, the Student will put one arm then the other arm through the armholes (the tutor will then lift the vest onto the Student's shoulders) with 75% accuracy in 3 out of 4 trials as documented in progress assessment results.

190.	By June, with verbal and hand over guidance, STUDENT will be able to, when attempting to tie shoes: 1) cross the laces and pull them tight 2) make a loop with the lace for one hand 3) make a loop with the other hand 4) swoop one lace under and the other lace over and 5) pull the loops tight, with 60% accuracy in 3 out of 4 trials as documented in progress assessment results.

191.	By June, with limited support, STUDENT will display proper letter formation when printing lower and upper case letters of the English alphabet, with 80% accuracy in 4 out of 5 trials, as documented in Student's log.

192.	By June, with prompting only as needed, STUDENT will use a switch to manipulate a variety of different items correctly, and independently remove his/her hands from the switch within 2 seconds, 70% of the time, in 4 out of 5 trials, as documented in Student's log.

193.	By June, STUDENT will independently use a three point pencil grip, in the classroom, 85% of the time in 4 out of 5 trials, as documented in Student's log.

194.	By June, STUDENT will independently print his/her name, including all letters in his/her name, and a space between the first and last name, when asked by his/her teacher, at least 80% of the time in 4 out of 5 trials, as documented in Student's log.

195. By June, STUDENT will be able to independently hold and use a crayon to colour for a minimum of 5 minutes, in the classroom, 90% of the time on 4 out of 5 trials, as documented in Student's log

196. By June, with reminders from a tutor, STUDENT will use scissors to cut, glue, paste, and/or colour (as assigned) 3 assignments, with a completion rate of 90% for 3 consecutive days over a 2 week period, as recorded in the Student's progress assessment reports.

197. By June, while using a pencil grip recommended by an OT, and with tutor prompting, STUDENT will be able to connect 80% of the dots on a worksheet,, without going outside of the intended pattern, in 4/5 trials, as documented in progress assessment results.

198. By June, while using loop scissors and with tutor prompting, STUDENT will be able to cut angles between 120 and 180 degrees and within a half centimeter of the indicated lines, with 80% accuracy in 7 of 10 trials, as documented in Student's log.

199. By June, with minimal tutor prompting, STUDENT will be able to print random letters of the alphabet neatly enough for his/her peers to be able to name the letters, 90% of the time in 4/5 trials, as documented in Student's log.

200. By June, with tutor assistance, STUDENT will be able to leave his/her pencil and crayons resting on his/her desk for 5 minutes, 90% of the time in 4/5 trials, as documented in Student's log.

201. By June, STUDENT will be able to independently protect him/herself by using the correct falling procedures (see attached sheet) in the classroom or anywhere in the school, 100% of the time 5 out of 5 days, as documented in progress assessment results.

202. By June, STUDENT will be able to, with the help of a tutor, practice a daily regimen of 10 minutes of exercise (including wall push-ups, ball roll on body, chair push-ups, bouncing a ball, sensory motor play with water, flashlight, and slip and slide) at least 90% of the time in 4 out of 5 days, as documented in Student's log.

203. By June, with physical assistance from a tutor, STUDENT will develop independence in maintaining optimal hearing aid use with at least 65% accuracy as outlined in the Hearing Aid Checklist in 3 out of 5 trials.

204. Provided with tutor supervision of occupational therapy 2-3 times per week, by June, STUDENT will have demonstrated increased sensory modulation as indicated

by decreasing observation of the 10 behaviors listed in the Adolescent Sensory Processing Checklist - Sensory Modulation, 80% of the time in 4 out of 5 trials, as documented in Student's log.

Personal and Social Well-being

205.   By June, STUDENT will respond to social cues, 90% of the time in 4 out of 5 trials, as documented in Student's log.

206.   By June, STUDENT will independently identify when he/she is experiencing high anxiety and signal the teacher or tutor for support, 90% of the time in 4 out of 5 trials, as documented in Student's log.

207.   By June, STUDENT will independently line up for recess, without inappropriate touching of other Students, 90% of the time on 4 out of 5 trials, as documented in Student's log.

208.   By June, STUDENT will independently practice restraint (see attached sheet) in responding to negative situations, 85% of the time in 9 out of 10 trials, as documented in Student's log.

209.   By June, STUDENT will be able to independently walk to and from the washroom, within a reasonable time frame, 90% of the time on 4/5 trials, as documented in Student's log.

210.   By June, STUDENT will initiate a play activity with a peer, using tutor support ,3 times a week 90% of the time on 4/5 trials, as documented in Student's log.

211.   By June, STUDENT will sit with his/her peers during circle time activities for a minimum of 15 minutes with tutor assistance, 90% of the time on 4/5 trials, as documented in Student's log.

212.   By June, without supervision, STUDENT will leave food on the ground and in the garbage, and not steal other Students food 90% of the time on 4/5 trials, as documented in Student's log.

213.   By June, STUDENT will participate to the best of his/her ability P-A-A type classes for a minimum of 10 minutes, on a daily basis as part of a whole class activity, 90% of the time 9 out of 10 days, as documented in Student's log.

214.   By June, with the assistance of a tutor, STUDENT will ask a Student to join him/her and the tutor for read aloud time with a tutor, with an accuracy rate of 75% for 3 consecutive days over a 2 week period, as documented in Student's log.

215.   By June, with the assistance of a tutor, STUDENT will name the emotions: happy, sad, excited, afraid, surprised, and angry, from face cards with an accuracy of 75% in 3 out of 4 trials, as documented in Student's log.

216.   By June, with tutor assistance, STUDENT will use a puppet to demonstrate 3 rules for personal safety in various situations with an accuracy of 75%, in 3 out of 4 trials, as documented in Student's log.

217.   By June, with the assistance of a tutor, STUDENT will shake the hand of a resource teacher, tutor, and principal upon arrival each morning, with an accuracy of 75% in 4 out of 5 situations, as documented in Student's log.

218.   By June, STUDENT will be able to work independently for 15 minutes, with minimal assistance with the use of picture cues / SEE, with 85% accuracy, on 4 out of 5 situations, as documented in Student's log.

219.   By June, with the use of visual aids and videos, STUDENT will be able to state and demonstrate key personal care requirements, with 90% accuracy on 4 out of 5 trials, as documented in Student's log.

220.   By June, STUDENT will be able to match PECS symbols with his/her basic wants and needs (food, drink, bathroom, toy, color, etc.), with minimal assistance 4 out of 5 times over a 2 week trial, as documented in Student's log.

221.   By June, STUDENT will independently be able to prepare a sandwich safely, and clean up afterwards, with at least 80% accuracy in 4 out of 5 trials in the school kitchen, as documented in Student's log.

222.   By June, STUDENT will, without prompting, ask a peer to play or join in his/her group (during recess and lunch hour), 4 out of 5 times for 5 consecutive days, as documented in Student's log.

223.   By June, STUDENT will independently choose from a list of self-control techniques displayed on the inside of his binder (either taking 3 deep breaths, counting to 5, thinking calm thoughts or going for a walk) , and follow one of these techniques 90% of the time, in 4 out of 5 trials, as documented in Student's log.

224.   By June, STUDENT will be able to independently maintain a conversation with a peer, inside the classroom about an academic topic, using appropriate language, in 4 out of 5 trials for a minimum of 5 minutes, 90% of the time, as documented in Student's log.

225. By June, STUDENT will be able to independently maintain a conversation about a preferred topic with an adult, for a minimum of 10 exchanges in 8 out of 10 trials over a two week period, with 80% accuracy, as documented in an academic behavior log.

226. By June, with a tutor monitor, STUDENT will write and send a message through email with a pre-determined Green Lake Student, with 90% accuracy, in 4 out of 5 consecutive school days.

227. By June, STUDENT will be able to independently add/count combinations of coins up to one dollar, in 4 out of 5 trials with 95% accuracy, as documented in Student's log..

228. By June, STUDENT will independently be able to tell the correct time to the minute, in 4 out of 5 trials with 90% accuracy, as documented in Student's log.

229. By June, STUDENT will demonstrate peer level social skills (see attached sheet) with a group of classmates through a cooperative board game, designed to be played by teams competing against each other, with 80% accuracy in 3 out of 4 trials, as documented in Student's log.

230. By June, STUDENT will, with minimal supervision from the classroom teacher and tutor, participate in an academic group activity in the classroom, using turn taking and using peer-level language, for a 30 minute period, with an 80% success rate, in 4 out of 5 trials, as documented in Student's log.

231. By June, without support, STUDENT, when experiencing difficulty on a learning task, will follow a basic 3 step problem solving procedure(please see attached steps), and be respectful with his/her teacher, tutor, and classmates, 80% of the time, in 7 out of 10 trials, as documented in Student's log.

232. By June, STUDENT will independently raise his/her hand in class and ask the teacher or tutor for help at least twice per day, with 90% accuracy in 4 of 5 situations, as documented in Student's log.

233. By June, STUDENT will, when frustrated or angry, independently use a strategy from a list of self-control techniques (5 deep breaths, positive self-talk, self-time out) 90% of the time in 4 of 5 episodes, as documented in Student's log.

234. By June, without support, STUDENT will have participated in extracurricular sports or other school based activities offered by the school, 4 out of 5 times a week, over a 2 week period, as documented in Student's log.

235. By June, STUDENT , with fidelity and tutor prompting, will have at least one positive, independent social interaction with a peer buddy, during the school day, for at least 10 minutes a day over 8 of 10 days, as documented in Student's log.

236. By June, STUDENT will independently participate in a minimum 10 minute small group activity and initiate a verbal response when asked questions by fellow Students, 80% in 5 of 5 trials, as documented in Student's log.

237. By June, STUDENT will be able to independently be able to contact emergency services (Social Services, RCMP, Health / Emergency Services, Kid Help Line) with 80% accuracy in 4 out of 5 trials, as documented in Student's log.

238. By June, STUDENT will be provided with the necessary support to independently attend school, unless sick or away, 80% of the time in 4 out of 5 days, as documented in Student's log.

239. By June, with limited supervision, STUDENT will prepare soup for consumption from can to stave to bowl, 100% of the time in 5 out of 5 trials, as documented in Student's log.

240. By June, with limited supervision, STUDENT will independently prepare a sandwich for personal consumption with 100% accuracy in 5 of 5 trials, in the home ec room, as documented in Student's log

241. By June, with limited visual prompts, STUDENT will match 12 core emotions (frustrated, calm, embarrassed, excited, scared, happy, lonely, nervous, confused, sad, surprised, angry) with facial expressions, and briefly describe these 12 core emotions, with 90% accuracy in 4 of 5 trials, as documented in Student's log.

242. By June, with occasional prompting, STUDENT will enter the gym for recreational fun, prior to the start of school, 80% of the time in 4 out of 5 trials, as documented in Student's log.

243. By June, in the classroom, STUDENT will be able to, when approached by a peer with a greeting (and tutor only a passive observer), respond to the peer with a similar verbal greeting, gesture, or picture pointing, 80% of the time in 4 of 5 trials, as documented in Student's log.

244. By June, during small group activities in the classroom, with occasional prompts, STUDENT will interact with his/her peers, at least 3 out of 5 times in 4 out of 5 trials, as documented in Student's log

245.   By June, STUDENT will independently voice his opinion/ideas when participating in cooperative groups, 80% of the time on 4 group projects out of 5,as documented in Student's log.

246.   By June, when participating in class discussions, STUDENT will independently speak in a voice loud enough for the class to hear, 4 out of 5 times on 4 out of 5 days, as documented in Student's log.

247.   By June, with periodic prompts, STUDENT will demonstrate increased competence in interpersonal relationship skills with peers, 4 out of 5 times, in at least 4 out of 5 trials, using anecdotal documentation.

248.   By June, STUDENT will facilitate positive mental health, by working with mental health professionals, in sessions at least 90% of the time, using anecdotal documentation.

249.   By June, with frequent prompting, STUDENT will select and use stress reducing strategies, in order to promote positive mental health, 80% of the time in 8 out of 10 trials, as documented in Student's log.

250.   By June, with verbal directions from the resource teacher, STUDENT will complete oral and written social language/skill/self-esteem assignments using themes from the Virtues program with at least 60% accuracy, in 3 out of 5 trials, as documented in Student's log.

251.   By June, with occasional prompts, STUDENT will leave the classroom to calm down in a pre-arranged space, when feeling frustrated in class, 80% of the time in 4 out of 5 trials, as documented in Student's log

252.   By the end of June, STUDENT will independently determine what response shows empathy by responding in a caring manner when someone is hurt or upset, with 90% accuracy in 9 out of 10 situations, as documented in Student's log.

253.   By June, STUDENT will independently initiate play with at least 1 Student from the class, in 2 out of 3 recesses on 4 out of 5 consecutive days, as documented in Student's log.

254.   By June, STUDENT will independently put on and keep on a monocular around his/her neck, so it is readily available for use to see objects at a distance, 90% of the time on 4 consecutive day out of 5,as documented in Student's log.

34

255. By June, with verbal support, STUDENT will use appropriate replacement behaviors (see attached sheet), when expressing anger or frustration, 90% of the time in 4 out of 5 situations, as documented in Student's log.

256. By June, with demonstration and support from a tutor, STUDENT will participate in special Olympic sports, achieving at least 50% of the Special Olympics checklist in 3 out of 5 trials.

257. By June, with verbal directions from the tutor, STUDENT will participate in the Life Skills Program, achieving at least 50% in the Community Based Life Skills Checklist, in 3 out of 5 trials.

258. By June, STUDENT will have completed 8 out of 10 life skills activities presented by Health Care (home care) with 80% accuracy, as documented in Student's log.

259. By June, with verbal reminders from the teacher and tutor, and with telephone follow-up contact from the resource teacher, STUDENT will attend at least 3 of 5 mental health counseling appointments with the social worker, 90% of the time, as documented in Student's log

260. By June, with verbal reminders from the tutor, STUDENT will complete at least 3 out of 5 computer assignments in the Career Cruising web site, with at least 60% accuracy in the Career Cruising Checklist.

261. By June, STUDENT will have participated in a minimum of 10 out of 20 activities or events organized by the Special Olympics Committee, as documented in Student's log.

262. By June, STUDENT will have completed 20 out of 30 self-esteem building exercises with aid from a Student support worker, working 1:1 once a week, as documented in Student's log.

263. By June, with verbal and visual reminders, STUDENT will be able to, when asked by a teacher or tutor, comply with a request within a 2 minute time frame without hesitating, in 4 out of 5 requests, as documented in Student's log.

264. By June, with verbal reminders from the resource teacher and tutor, and follow up from the addictions prevention and recovery counselor, STUDENT will attend at least 3 out of 5 addictions and recovery counseling appointments as indicated in the Contact Log 100% of the time, in 4 out of 5 situations, as documented in Student's log.

265. By June, STUDENT will independently engage in 2 of the following 3 activities with a classmate - throw and catch a ball, build a tower with blocks and alternately take turns putting on blocks, and roll a car back and forth across a table, 90% of the time, 4 out of 5 days, as documented in Student's log.

266. By June, STUDENT will independently engage in 3 of the following 4 activities with one classmate - throw and catch a ball, play a game of snakes and ladders, build a tower with linking cubes, or roll a toy car back and forth across a table, 90% of the time, 4 out of 5 days, as documented in Student's log.

267. By June, with verbal reminders from a tutor, STUDENT will circle 4 out of 7 good personal care practices listed in the "Developing Independence in Personal Care Checklist, with at least 60% accuracy in 3 out of 5 trials, as documented in Student's log.

268. By June, with occasional tutor assistance, STUDENT will actively participate in 3 of 4 self-esteem builder lessons, 90% of the time, 4 out of 5 days, as documented in Student's log.

269. By June, STUDENT will independently say "no, this is dangerous", using pictures as guides when asked to do something dangerous in a role play situation with a minimum of 2 of the following 6 people - Student support worker, resource teacher, principal, classroom teacher, tutor, or unfamiliar teacher, 90% of the time, 4 out of 5 days, as documented in Student's log.

270. By June, with verbal reminders from a tutor, STUDENT will complete 90% of the personal care hygiene and department tasks, as indicated in the Developing Independence in Personal Care Checklist, 90% of the time, in 3 out of 5 trials, as documented in Student's log.

271. By June, with verbal corrections from a tutor, STUDENT will independently demonstrate 4 personal care skills listed in the Developing Independence in Personal Care Checklist, with at least 60% accuracy in 3 out of 5 trials, as documented in Student's log.

272. By June, STUDENT will independently explain the consequences of a "what will happen if" scenario in 4 out of 5 social stories read aloud by teacher, tutor, or Student support worker, 90% of the time, in 4 out of 5 trials, as documented in Student's log.

273. By June, when becoming visibly upset, STUDENT will be able to, with tutor prompting when needed, choose an effective strategy and calm down within 5 minutes, 90% of the time, in 4 out of five episodes, as recorded in tutor's daybook.

274. By June, STUDENT will participate in a tutor directed play activity with a selected group of peers, for a minimum of 5 minutes without wandering away, 90% of the time, in 4 out of 5 trials, as documented in Student's log.

275. By June, STUDENT will independently participate in a group activity with peers in the classroom for a minimum of 20 minutes at least 80% of the time in 4 of 5 group activities, as documented in Student's log.

276. By June, with limited prompting, STUDENT will effectively demonstrate 5 age appropriate social skills (see attached sheet), appropriate language, and demonstrate appropriate behavior, when interacting with the teacher, tutor, other adults, and peers within the school, 80% of the time, 4 out of 5 consecutive days, as documented in Student's log.

277. By June, with limited verbal prompting, STUDENT will be able to keep his/her hands to self and be without incident of assaulting other Students or destroying school property in all situations, 100% of the time 5 of 5 days, as documented in Student's log.

278. By June, with limited prompting, when a peer or adult greets STUDENT, he/she will independently extend their hand out and slap, touch, or shake hands with that person, at least 80% of the time in 4 out of 5 trials.

279. By June, STUDENT will participate in a learning game, in the classroom setting with his/her peers, taking a turn the same as other participants in the game and wait to take a turn, with 80% accuracy in 4 out of 5 games played.

280. By the end of June, STUDENT will be able to independently and accurately match the oral names of animals (bear, moose, fish, deer, bird), food (apple, toast, cereal, sandwich, pizza, potatoes), and primary colors by pointing to the appropriate pictures, when displaced in a group of no less than 4 pictures, 75% of the time in 4 out of 5 trials, as documented in Student's log.

281. By June, with frequent prompts by the teacher or tutor, STUDENT will demonstrate the positive social skills of: 1) appropriate use of personal space, 2) avoiding inappropriate touch of others, and 3) not interrupting but taking turn in the

conversation, with peers, in the classroom 80% of the time in 4 of 5 reported situations

282. By June, STUDENT will have participated in his/her mental health counseling sessions with a professional mental health worker, 90% of scheduled sessions

283. By June, with occasional verbal prompts, STUDENT will have enhanced his/her conversational skills by maintaining a conversation with peers 80% of the time, in the classroom, as documented in progress report results.

284. By June, with occasional verbal prompts, STUDENT will use stress reducing strategies (may include but not limited to: self-calming strategies, self-time out safe area in the school, leaving class to talk to school social worker, calling mother or grandparents) 80% in 8 out of 10 situations, as documented in progress assessment results.

285. By June, with verbal directions from a tutor, STUDENT will participate in daily Special Olympics (SO) fitness, sport and recreation activities in the SO Active School Based Program at least 50% in 3 out of 5 situations.

286. By June, physically accompanied by a tutor and follow up by resource teacher telephone liaison with Addictions Preventions and recovery and mental health workers, STUDENT will attend appointments set up by the Clinic with at least 60% attendance of scheduled meetings.

287. By June, STUDENT will independently engage in 3 of the following 4 activities with a classmate - work cooperatively on an art and craft activity, throw and catch a ball, play with a train set, roll a toy car back and forth across the floor, 90% of the time in 4 out of 5 days, as documented in the Log for Intensive Support.

288. By June, with encouragement from a tutor, in the classroom, STUDENT will engage in play with various sensory toys with a classmate, a minimum of 10 minutes, 4 out of 5 days.

289. By June, with occasional tutor assistance, STUDENT will actively participate in 4 out of 6 self-esteem builder lessons, 90% of the time, 4 out of 5 days, as documented in a Log for Intensive Support.

290. By June, when becoming upset, STUDENT will be able to calm him/herself down, and experience a maximum of 2 outbursts per week, 90% of the time, 4 out of 5 weeks, as recorded in the Student's behavior log.

291. By June, STUDENT will, after given verbal support and caring explanation of what is expected of him/her, will accept consequences, without protest, at least 80% of the time, in 4 of 5 situations, as documented in Student's behaviour log.

292. By June, STUDENT will be able to follow all steps of personal hygiene after using the washroom (steps include: using toilet paper, flushing the toilet, and washing hands) at least 90% of the time, in 4 out of 5 trials, as reported on a self-reporting hygiene checklist.

293. By June, in the classroom, when not able to hear teacher instructions in the classroom, STUDENT will be able to advocate for him/herself and either ask the teacher to turn on the FM sound field system or move to a different location in the classroom, in order to hear instructions more clearly, 100 % of the time, on 5 out of 5 situations, as recorded in the Student's data log.

294. By June, in the classroom, STUDENT will be able to work in a small group setting for up a 15 minute period, without getting upset (causing a disruption/argument or leaving the situation) 80% of the time in 4 out of 5 trials.

295. By June, STUDENT will be able to identify familiar school voices and use the school names of: all satellite teachers, dental staff, office staff, and community school staff, and all playground supervisors at least 90% of the time, as documented in the Student's data log.

296. By June, STUDENT will actively participate in a small group and partner activity, with a maximum of 3 peer coaching prompts, keeping on topic for a minimum least 10 minute period and not becoming visibly uncomfortable, 90% of the time, in 4 out of 5 trials, as documented in the Student's data log.

297. By June, with verbal directions from a tutor, STUDENT will participate in daily Special Olympics (SO) fitness, sport and recreation activities in the SO Active School Based Program 90% of the time, in 3 out of 5 trials, as documented in Student's log.

298. By June, with limited verbal prompting, STUDENT will independently respond appropriately to peer teasing or bullying, by choosing the appropriate choice as follows: 1) stop and count to 5, 2) ignore, 3) verbally express how you feel, 4) give reasons to stop, 100% of the time in 4 out of 5 situations, as documented in assessment results.

299. By June, with limited assistance, STUDENT will be able to use a cookbook (Company Coming) and bake 10 healthy food recipes from scratch, 80% of the time, in 4 out of 5 trials, as documented in Student's log.

300. By June, STUDENT will be able to independently initiate and maintain a conversation with a female peer, for up to 15 minutes, about an age appropriate topic, and using appropriate language, 80% of the time in 4 out of 5 situations, as documented in the Student's behavior log.

301. By June, under direct supervision, STUDENT will be able to mix and administer his/her prescribed medication by him/herself on time, and with the assistance of a teacher or tutor, 100% of the time in 5 out of 5 situations, as documented in medicine administration log.

302. By June, with limited support, STUDENT will recognize the feelings of frustration and will choose a method from a list below and consistently calm down, at least 80% of the time in 4 out of 5 situations, as documented in Student's behavior log. (List of strategies include: body breaks, time outs, counting to 5, deep breathing, and relaxations techniques)

303. By June, STUDENT will, without being monitored, eat only food that is provided for him/her 90% of the time, on 4 out of 5 trials, as documented in Student's log.

304. By June, with assistance from a tutor, STUDENT will be able to identify 4 emotions (happy, sad, upset, angry) from a choice of several faces with various expressions, at least 75% of the time, in 4 out of 5 trials, as documented in Student's log..

305. By June, with the assistance of a tutor, STUDENT will develop positive and self-help decision making skills (see attached sheet) with 70% accuracy in 4 out of 5 trials, as documented in Student's log.

306. By June, STUDENT will be able to recite personal information about him/her with 95% accuracy, 4 out of 5 consecutive times, as documented in progress assessment results, as documented in Student's log.

307. By June, STUDENT will independently complete a fishing activity in a small group 100% of the time, in 4 out of 5 small group fishing situations, as documented in progress assessment.

308. By June, STUDENT will have joined a club or sports team of interest, and participate at least 80% of the time, in 4 out of 5 meetings or practices per month, independently as documented in progress assessment.

309. By June, STUDENT with fidelity and tutor prompting, will have at least one positive, hands off, social interaction with a buddy, during the school day, for at least 10 minutes, 4/5 days a week, as documented in progress assessment results.

310. By June, with tutor prompting and while playing a letter recognition activity, STUDENT will wait to touch the SMART Board by staying at his/her seat, until the Student before him/her has gone back to their seat, at least 80% of the time in 4/5 trials, as documented in progress assessment results.

311. By June, STUDENT will participate in at least one large group activity during class time, when prompted by a teacher/tutor at least 90% of the time in 5/5 trials, as documented in progress assessment results.

. Work in small group w/ little problem
, Use stress reducing strategies
. Calming techniques
, Appropriate response to peer teasing
. Hands to himself

Transition

312. By June, STUDENT will independently transition, with the help of a visual schedule and be prepared for new subjects 90% of the time on 4 out of 5 days, as documented in Student's log.

313. By June, STUDENT will independently walk quietly down the hallway with his classmates, keeping his hands to himself 90% of the time on 4/5 trials, as documented in Student's log.

314. By June, STUDENT will independently transition, with the help of a visual schedule and be prepared for new subjects 90% of the time on 4 out of 5 days, as documented in Student's log.

315. By June, STUDENT will nod (affirmative or negative) to indicate his safety when being loaded or unloaded on the van lift, 90% of the time on 4/5 trials when prompted by the Student assistant worker, as documented in Student's log.

316. By June, STUDENT will transition from outside the school building to inside the school without fussing 90% of the time in 4 out of 5 trials, as documented in Student's log.

317. By June, STUDENT will be successfully cued by a time-timer, and the use of a visual schedule and be prepared for his next class with the correct scribbler, books, etc. with 95% accuracy, in 4 out of 5 trials, as documented in Student's log.

318. By June, STUDENT will be able to manage time independently, so that he/she is able to change from one activity to another on his/her timetable, with 90% accuracy 4 out of 5 consecutive times, as documented in Student's log..

319. By June, STUDENT will be able to, with assistance, help canteen workers take orders and give change with 85 % accuracy, in 4 out of 5 trials, as documented in Student's log.

320. By June, STUDENT will learn to successful change activities for gym time, computer time, and snack time when prompted using PECS pictures, 4 out of 5 times over a two week trial, as documented in Student's log.

321. By June, when the bell rings for the 5 minute break between classes, STUDENT will manage her time of going to his/her locker, washroom, or drinking fountain, and move to class and be sitting at his/her desk, when the bell rings to start class, 2 out

of 3 times per day over a week period 100% of the time, as documented in Student's log.

322. By June 2010, when provided with a 3 minute warning using a visual schedule, STUDENT will follow the direction to change activities in the classroom setting, at least 8 out of 10 times 4 out of 5 consecutive days, as documented in Student's log.

323. By June, STUDENT will be able to independently transition from a nonacademic task to an academic task in 4 out of 5 trials, with 80% accuracy, as documented in Student's log.

324. By June, STUDENT will be able to independently move from classroom to classroom, in 4 out of 5 period changes, during a 1 week cycle, with 80% accuracy, as documented in an academic behaviour log.

325. By June, STUDENT will independently move from classroom to classroom without incident, in 4 out of 5 periods over a one week trial, as documented in Student's log.

326. By June, STUDENT will successfully participate in a 30 minute instructional cycle, demonstrating 20 minutes of on task behavior followed by a 10 minute body break 3 out of 5 times a day with 90% accuracy, as documented in Student's log.

327. By June, STUDENT will independently arrive at his/her first class after lunch hour on time, 4 out of 5 days during a five day week, 90% of the time, as documented in Student's log.

328. By June, STUDENT will independently begin a newly presented activity in class, with minimal prompting, and stay on task for a minimum of 5 minutes without prompting, with 90% accuracy in 4 out of 5 trials, as documented in Student's log.

329. By June, STUDENT will independently return to class after a bathroom break, within a maximum of 5 minutes, 80% of the time, 4 out of 5 days, as documented in Student's log.

330. By June, STUDENT will independently attend the coat rack area, classroom work stations, and school computer room, with minimal visual supervision from the tutor, without incidents of misbehavior, 90% of the time on 4 of 5 trials, as documented in Student's log.

331. By June, STUDENT will, when the bell rings, independently gather his/her things from that period and put them away, and get the books and supplies out for the

next class period, prior to the start of a lesson, with 80% success rate over 5 days of classes, as documented in Student's log.

332. By June, STUDENT will with tutor assistance, will at the end of the day, be ready (getting outside cloths on, homework etc.) and wait outside 5 minutes, early in preparation for the special education van to pick him/her up for home time, with 100% accuracy in 5 out of 5 trials, as documented in Student's log.

333. By June, with occasional prompts, STUDENT will transition from subject to subject, and place to place, by being on time and being prepared for class, 80% of the time in 8 out of 10 trials, as documented in Student's log.

334. By June, with occasional prompts and the use a visual timer, STUDENT will review and follow a set of expectations for each transition period in school with 80% accuracy in 5 of 5 trials, as documented in Student's log.

335. By June, with periodic verbal prompts, STUDENT will gather his/her homework, be dressed for outside, and arrive 5 minutes early in front of the school ready to get the school bus for home 100 % of the time, in 10 out of 10 trials, as documented in Student's log.

336. By June, with period prompts, STUDENT will independently put his books and scribblers away at the end of a subject period, and take out relevant materials (text, scribbler, pen, etc.) for next class, in 4 out of 5 trials, with 80% accuracy, as documented in Student's log.

337. By June, when provided with a 2 minute warning, using a picture schedule, STUDENT will follow the required directions to prepare for satellite classes, 90% of the time, in at least 4 out of 5 consecutive days, as documented in Student's log.

338. By June, with occasional prompts, STUDENT will employ the skills necessary for success in jr. high school structure and routines, 90% of the time, on a 4 of 5 day trial, as documented in Student's log. (These skills include: interacting with teacher, tutor, classmates, and organization of materials required for each class, etc.)

339. By June, STUDENT will independently keep his/her desk and work space organized by putting papers/books into proper places, after each class subject, 90% of the time, on 4 out of 5 consecutive days, as documented in Student's log.

340. By June, STUDENT will independently continue working on assigned work in class, until directed by the teacher to stop, 90% of the time on 4 consecutive days out of 5, as documented in Student's log.

341. By June, with occasional prompts, STUDENT will demonstrate the skills necessary for success in grade 10 both in structure and routine, 90% of the time, in at least 4 out of 5 trials, as documented in Student's log.

342. By June, using verbal prompts, STUDENT will ask a tutor for physical support when walking through the school hallways to get to classes, less than 60% of time, in 3 out of 5 trials, using an ask for help to walk checklist, as documented in Student's log.

343. By June, with occasional prompting, STUDENT will complete the required transition requirements (see attached schedule) from one subject to another within 5 minutes of the end of the previous class, with 80% accuracy in 4 out of 5 trials, as documented in Student's log.

344. By June, STUDENT will independently return to class after using the bathroom, within 2 minutes after leaving class, 90% of the time, 4 out of 5 days, as documented in Student's log.

345. By June, STUDENT will, with verbal prompts and physical support, get his/her jacket on by pushing up arms into sleeves, 50% of the time in 5 out of 5 trials, as documented in Student's log.

346. By June, STUDENT will independently follow school routines when the bell rings to indicate that recess time is over, 90% of the time 4 out of 5 days, as documented in Student's log.

347. By June, with verbal directions from the tutor, STUDENT will make walking transitions between classes without incident 90% of the time, at least 3 out of 5 days, as indicated in the Transition Checklist.

348. By June, with the aid of a visual timer and tutor support, STUDENT will put away work from previous assignments and start new assignments within 3 minutes in 6 periods of 8, over a 3-5 day period, 90% of the time, as documented in Student's log.

349. By June, in the classroom, using a timer and visual prompting, STUDENT will be able to, after a 5 minute advanced warning, put away an activity, and get ready for the next activity within 1 minute, 80% of the time in 4 out of 5 trials, as documented in Student's log.

350. By June, STUDENT will independently put away the activity he/she is working on and get out the next activity when the classroom teacher says it is time to do the next activity, 90% of the time, 4 out of 5 days, as documented in Student's log.

351.	By June, STUDENT will independently retell instructions to tutor, with 90% accuracy, 4 out of 5 days, as documented in Student's log.

352.	By June, with verbal reminders from a tutor, STUDENT will remember needed supplies i.e. a pencil, proper scribbler, required texts, and other supplies, 80% of the time in 3 out of 5 trials, as documented in Student's log.

353.	By June, when a change has been made to the daily schedule, STUDENT will use self-talk 60% of the time, to calm down and accept the change within a 2 minute period, in 4 out of 5 instances, as recorded in a tutor's day planner.

354.	By June, in the classroom, STUDENT will be able to, independently take his/her agenda book home to show parents and return it back to school, 90% of the time in 4 out of 5 school days, as documented in Student's log.

355.	By June, STUDENT will be able to adequately prepare for class by taking out the appropriate books and scribblers requested by the teacher, with minimum prompts, 90% of the time in 5 out of 5 trials, as documented in Student's log.

356.	By June, when preparing for home time, STUDENT will pack all necessary items for home in order to successfully complete homework and fill out agenda independently with 90% accuracy in 4 out of 5 days, as documented in Student's log.

357.	By June, with limited support, and using a visual timer and cueing system, STUDENT will take no longer than 5 minutes to transition from one task to a complete other task, with 90% accuracy, 4 out of 5 times, as documented in Student's log.

358.	By June, STUDENT will independently put his/her outdoor shoes and outdoor clothing neatly in a proper locker space, with 90% accuracy in 9 out of 10 occasions (after recess or returning after lunch), as documented in Student's log.

359.	By June, STUDENT will be able to name 5 staff members and locate 5 areas of the school, when taken on a walk about around the school, 90% of the time in 4 out of 5 trials, as documented in the Student's data log.

360.	By June, STUDENT will, with visual supports, be able to follow a change in routine (by listening to the instruction and asking for clarification if needed) and follow the instruction of the teacher or tutor, at least 80% of the time, as documented in the Student's data log.

361. By June, when changes are required in the Student's day, STUDENT will utilize a taught strategy (see attached strategies) so that he/she may calm themselves and accept the changes to occur, within a maximum 5 minute period, in 4 out of 5 instances, 80% of the time, as documented in Student's log.

362. By June, in the classroom, STUDENT will independently fill out his/her agenda, take it home daily and return it the next day, successfully completing all assigned homework tasks recorded in the agenda, 80% of the time 4 out of 5 days, as documented in the Student's data log.

363. By June, STUDENT will, at recess on the playground, with advanced warning and picture support, come in to the school after the bell, within a 2 minute time period, at least 90% of the time, unassisted in 4 out of 5 trials, as documented in Student's log.

364. By June, STUDENT will be able to independently walk down the hallway to his/her satellite class or to his/her recess job, at least 80% of the time, without incident, 4 out of 5 consecutive days, as documented in Student's log.

365. By June, STUDENT will be able to independently be able to remember necessary items to bring to school to and from home each day, by taking his/her agenda book home, review for reminders, have it signed by parents, and then bring it back to school, 90% of the time in 4 out of 5 days, as documented in the Student's data log.

366. By June, with tutor and teacher support, STUDENT will have explored 5 career options with 80% completion of course materials for each career option, as documented in Student's completion checklist.

367. By June, STUDENT will transition from a wheelchair to mat to standing on a table lift, without fussing, 90% of the time in 4 out of 5 trials, as documented in Student's log.

368. By June, STUDENT will independently get to his/her work placement on time, 90% of the time, over a consecutive 5 day period, as documented in Student's log.

369. By June, STUDENT will complete 90% of his/her non-preferred assignments in ELA, during the allotted time period for a task, in 5/5 trials, as measured in an assessment worksheet, over a 5 day period, as documented in Student's log.

370. By June, STUDENT will independently transition to a new assignment in the classroom, 80% of the time, in 4 out of 5 trials, as measured by an assessment checklist, over a 5 day period.

371. By June, STUDENT will independently return to class within 4 minutes after a bathroom break 90% of the time, in 7 out of 10 consecutive bathroom breaks, as documented in Student's log.

372. By June, independently, STUDENT will be able to remain on task in the classroom, when completing non preferred work, for minimum 40 minute duration, 80% of the time in 4 of 5 school periods, over 4 to 5 days, as documented in Student's log.

373. By June, with fidelity, and the supervision of a tutor or teacher, STUDENT will be able to walk in a line with their classmates to Dene class at an appropriate pace, without incident, 100% of the time in 5 out of 5 trials, as documented in Student's log.

- Stay on task w/ non-preferred activity
- Bathroom break — within a specified time frame
- Get correct materials out in class
- Ask for clarifications in class
- Able to calm himself after schedule/routine change.

Bonus: Social Competency

1. By June 2012, the learner will be able to use a positive word selected from a visual chart to describe the events of the day at least four times out of six in a six day cycle.

2. By June during playtime, the student will engage in a short verbal exchange (at least 2 utterances) with a classmate without staff mediation in at least 4 play periods in one week.

3. Using behavior rating scale, student will rate a one in breakfast routine at least 6 out of 10 days with teacher intervention and cues by June, 2012.

4. By June 30, 2012, Student will say "excuse me" and wait for a social cue in at least 7 out of 10 times before beginning a conversation.

5. By the end of June, during break time, the student will approach teachers in conversations and wait without talking or interrupting beside them until they greet her at least 5/10 consecutive times.

6. When given positive feedback ("You did a good job"), and a verbal cue, ("Remember to be proud of your-self"), the student will respond with a positive statement such as, ("Thank-you"), in 5 out of 10 interactions, by the end of June/06.

7. The student will independently allow 3 feet of space between himself and an other person, 8/10 times, in familiar areas of the school and with familiar people, by the end of June.

8. By the end of the first semester and using an offer of helping with math, Student will independently initiate conversation with at least 2 students during his daily resource period at least 3 out of 5 resource periods in the week.

9. Student will say "thank-you" in response to 'good job, student's name" with a partial verbal prompt ("thank...") 4/5 times in 1 day.

10. To help the student have a successful recess the EA will review with him a plan for playing outside before he goes out. This plan will be with visuals in a story setting. By June 2012, the student will play with his designated toys without getting upset when other children come around 8 out of 10 recesses for 4 consecutive days.

Student Outcome Rubric

For this edition, the author has made available a Student Outcome Rubric you can use together with your SMART Goals. Find the downloads below:

http://www.chrisdefeyter.com/sor.pdf

Additionally, a checklist has been made available to check the construction of revised SMART Goals:

http://www.chrisdefeyter.com/checklist.pdf

IEP HelpDesk

For a limited time, you have the opportunity to connect to the author to customize one of your SMART Goals for one of your students. This includes

- Refining a SMART Goal
- a Simple strategy to go with a SMART Goal
- and answering one important question to get your student to achieve.

If you would like to get feedback and ask specific questions about your student, please go to the website, and complete the request form. If for some reason this link does not work, copy and paste the following in your browser:

http://fluidsurveys.com/s/iep-helpdesk-amazon/

Chris de Feijter

45235264R00031

Made in the USA
Lexington, KY
21 September 2015